# SCIENCE IN ACTION

# Electricity Turns the World On!

By Tom Johnston
Illustrated by Sarah Pooley

**Gareth Stevens Publishing**
**Milwaukee**

Library of Congress Cataloging-in-Publication Data

Johnston, Tom.
  Electricity turns the world on!

  (Science in action)
  Includes index.
  Summary: Illustrates the properties of electricity and its development as a vital energy source.
  1. Electricity--Juvenile literature. (1. Electricity) I. Pooley, Sarah, ill. II. Title. III. Series: Science in action
(Milwaukee, Wis.)
  QC527.2.J64  1988        537        87-42655
  ISBN 1-55532-435-5
  ISBN 1-55532-410-X (lib. bdg.)

North American edition first published in 1988 by

Gareth Stevens, Inc.   7317 West Green Tree Road
Milwaukee, Wisconsin 53223, USA

Hand lettering: Kathy Hall
Additional artwork on pages 17, 18, 19:  Sheri Gibbs
Typeset by Web Tech, Milwaukee
Project editor: Rhoda Sherwood

Technical consultants: Jonathan Knopp, Chair, Science Department, Rufus King High School, Milwaukee;
Willette Knopp, Reading Specialist and Elementary Teacher, Fox Point-Bayside (Wis.) School District.

2 3 4 5 6 7 8 9 93 92 91 90 89 88

What do thunderstorms, nuclear power stations, and combing your hair have in common?

They all produce electricity.

The discovery of electricity is probably the thing that has most changed our lives over the last few hundred years. People have been investigating electricity for over 2,500 years. About 600 BC, a Greek called Thales found that if he rubbed a piece of amber, he could make small objects stick to it. Amber is a sort of natural plastic, and you can do a similar experiment by rubbing a plastic pen and picking up small pieces of paper with it. About 1570 AD, William Gilbert, doctor to Queen Elizabeth I of England, carried out similar experiments. He named the effects that he saw *electricity*, after the Greek word for amber, *elektron*.

In 1733 a French scientist, Charles du Fay, tried this experiment.

If two amber beads are suspended on string and then rubbed...

...they repel each other and are driven apart.

The same happens with two glass beads.

But if one amber bead and one glass bead are rubbed and held close, they attract one another.

Mr. du Fay had discovered that there are two kinds of electric charge — positive and negative.

You can use this same rubbing effect to produce electric sparks. Wearing a nylon shirt and a woolen sweater, stand in a dark room in front of a mirror. Pull the sweater off. Sparks will fly between the shirt and the sweater.

These sparks are caused by electric charges leaping through the air. This is exactly what happens when you see lightning during thunderstorms. Inside clouds, there are tiny particles of water, ice, and air. The friction caused when these particles rub together builds up to form an electric charge. When a great number of charges collect, they can leap through the air as a large lightning spark. The sparks leap from cloud to cloud, or from a cloud to the ground. We now believe the spark can leap from the ground to the cloud as well.

Lightning can be dangerous and has been known to destroy trees, houses, and even people. In 1753, an American scientist, Benjamin Franklin, invented the lightning rod. He flew kites into thunderstorms in order to collect an electric charge along the line attached to each. He was lucky not to have been killed doing this.

Electricity flowed through the wet line.

Lightning is a giant electric spark. It carries a lot of energy and can be very dangerous. If trees or tall buildings are hit by lightning, they can be badly damaged.

When electricity reached the metal key, a spark was produced.

NEVER try anything like Benjamin Franklin's experiment. Electricity flowing through the kite string could kill you.

About 45 years later, an Italian scientist, Alessandro Volta, invented an easier way of producing electricity — the battery. He did this by putting a piece of paper, soaked in salt water, between two small pieces of metal — one copper and the other zinc. He attached a wire to each of these and placed the ends of the wires against his tongue. This made it tingle.

Volta then piled lots of the batteries on top of each other so that the copper piece of the one below touched the zinc piece of the one above. This gave off enough electricity to produce a spark when the ends of the wires were brought together.

Modern batteries are really just like Volta's. If you have a used-up 1.5-volt flashlight battery, cut it open to see what is inside. Once you have cut through the protective metal case, it will come apart fairly easily.

You will see it has a zinc case inside, just like Volta's piece of zinc, but instead of the piece of copper, it has a rod of carbon. Between the carbon and zinc, Volta's salt water has been replaced with an acid paste. Don't get the paste on your clothes, and wash your hands afterward, too.

This is a 1.5-volt battery or cell. A larger battery, such as a 9V one, is really just like six 1.5V cells joined together.

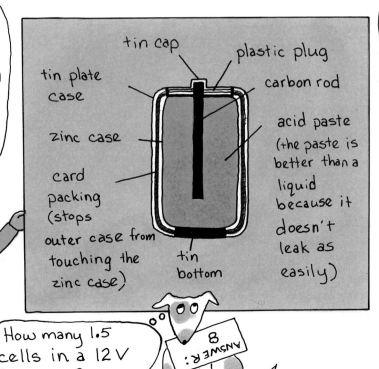

tin cap
plastic plug
tin plate case
carbon rod
zinc case
acid paste (the paste is better than a liquid because it doesn't leak as easily)
card packing (stops outer case from touching the zinc case)
tin bottom

How many 1.5 cells in a 12V battery?

ANSWER: 8

If you leave batteries in a radio or flashlight unused for a long time, they will leak and the acid will corrode the metal parts of the flashlight.

7

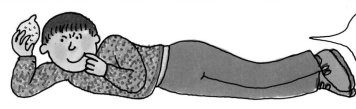

You can use the zinc and carbon from the battery to make some unusual batteries of your own. Using scissors, cut the zinc into one-third inch (1 cm) strips. You'll need several carbon rods, but you don't need to cut open more batteries for these. The lead inside pencils is really carbon, so you can use this instead. Now you need a lemon, two pieces of wire (any thin wire will do), and a small 1.5-volt bulb in a holder. Stick a piece of zinc and a carbon rod into the lemon, keeping them about three-quarters of an inch (2 cm) apart. Attach a wire to the top of each (paper clips are very useful for attaching wires), and then fix the other ends of the wires to your bulb holder, as shown in the diagram. The bulb should light up. The juice in the lemon acts just like Volta's salt water or the acid in a battery.

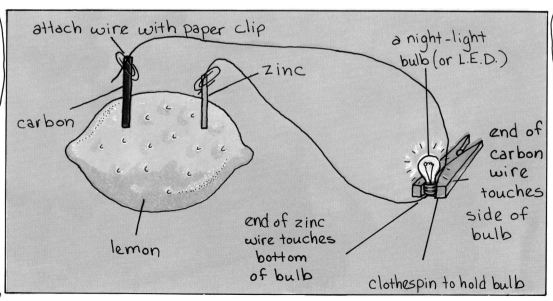

You could use a Light Emitting Diode (L.E.D.) instead of a light bulb. It needs less electric current to make it light up.

8

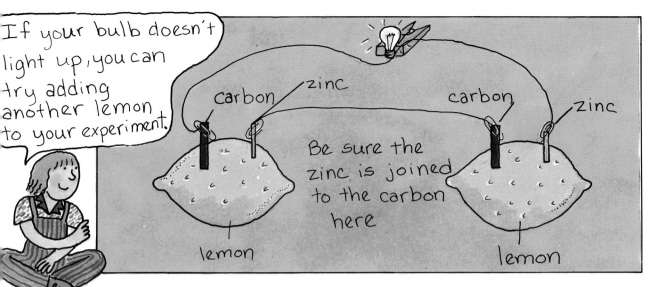

You can also do this experiment using potatoes, onions, apples, or oranges, instead of lemons. You would need three potatoes to light one L.E.D. and about ten potatoes to light one light bulb.

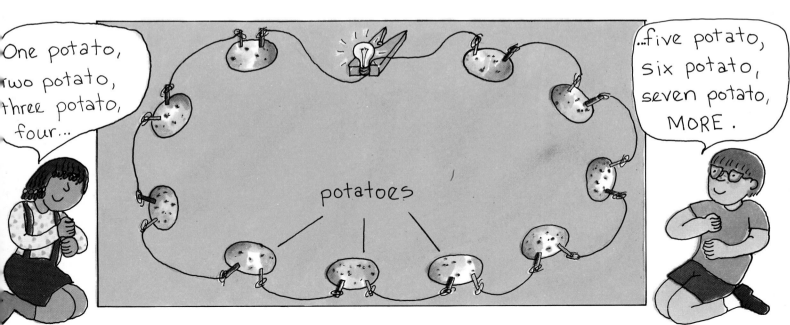

Fruit and vegetables are not the only things we can get electricity from. Some animals produce their own electricity. The electric catfish, the electric ray, and the electric eel, for example, can produce shocks that can stun or kill their prey. The South American electric eel can stun a horse as it crosses a river. Shocks from eels have been measured as high as 550 volts.

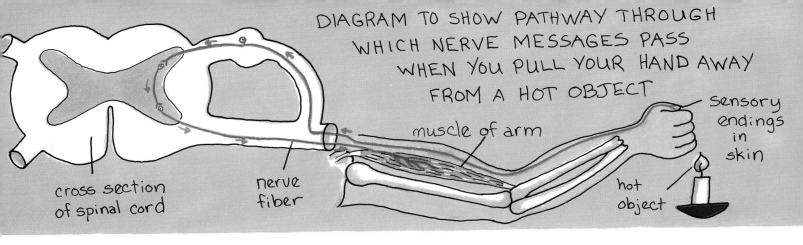

DIAGRAM TO SHOW PATHWAY THROUGH WHICH NERVE MESSAGES PASS WHEN YOU PULL YOUR HAND AWAY FROM A HOT OBJECT

Even your body can produce electricity.   In fact, it uses electricity to pass messages within it, in much the same way that a computer does.  Your nerves, which are long, thin fibers, can produce small electric charges that travel along one nerve and on to the next one — rather like electricity passing through wiring in a circuit.  These electric charges travel very fast.  If you step on a pin, the message from your foot takes only 1/20th of a second to reach your spinal cord, return to your foot, and make your muscle move the foot.  Your brain also produces tiny electric currents, but these are so tiny that it would take about 30 million of them to light up a small flashlight bulb.

💡 is the electrical symbol for a bulb.

Use it when you're drawing a diagram.

← A lazy artist

To make any battery work, you need to have a circuit. This is an unbroken length of wire that links one end of your battery, one terminal, to the other end.

You can show this with three wires, a 1.5-volt battery, and a 1.5-volt bulb. To hold the bulb, check your hardware or electronics store for a special socket that has screw-like prongs, called leads, that you can attach your wires to. Connect them to make a circuit and they will work, but leave a gap in the circuit anywhere and the bulb will not light up.

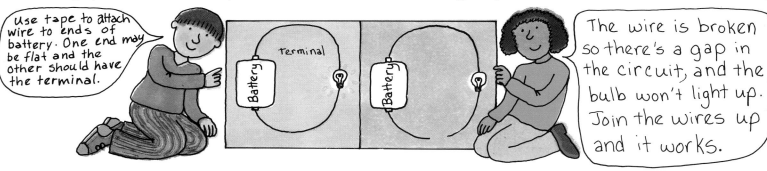

Use tape to attach wire to ends of battery. One end may be flat and the other should have the terminal.

Terminal

Battery

Battery

The wire is broken so there's a gap in the circuit, and the bulb won't light up. Join the wires up and it works.

This gap in the circuit can be quite useful as a switch for turning the circuit on or off.

When the switch is off, the contacts are open. There is a gap in the electrical circuit.

SWITCH

spring

Contacts open

Switch off

SWITCH

spring bends

contacts close

Switch on

When the switch is turned on, the spring bends, forcing the contacts to close. This makes a complete electrical circuit.

A French king, when experimenting with electricity, accidentally gave a shock to 700 monks who were joined hand-to-hand.

OOOOWWWW!

Electricity flows only through complete circuits and through certain substances. You can use a circuit with a gap to test which substances will let electricity pass through them. Set up your experiment like this:

If the bulb lights up, then electricity is getting through!

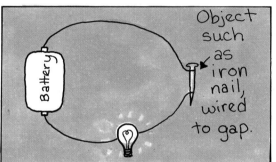

Battery

Object such as iron nail, wired to gap.

Try as many different things as you can find. Try paper, plastic, foil, pencil lead, etc.

Only recently have we come to understand exactly what electricity is. Everything is made up of tiny particles called atoms. Atoms themselves are made up of even smaller particles, and one of these smaller particles is called the electron. Electrons can break away from atoms, can move freely. Substances that let electricity flow through them have free electrons. This is the electricity flowing. It is a build-up of electrons on the surface of things that causes the sparks we mentioned earlier.

The most simple atom is the hydrogen atom. It has one electron in orbit around its nucleus.

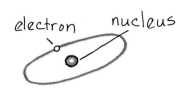

electron   nucleus

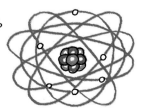

A carbon atom has six electrons circling the nucleus.

If something lets electricity pass through it, we call it a conductor. From the experiment on page 13, you probably found that most metals are conductors. Things like paper and plastic won't conduct very well, so we call them insulators. This is why electric wires are usually covered in plastic or rubber. The covering insulates the wire so that electricity cannot flow out of it into the things it touches.

We can use conductors and insulators to make an electrical game. This is a game board that needs a 1.5-volt battery and bulb. You also need two wires and some strips of aluminum foil for conductors. You can use tape as an insulator.

The front of the board has questions down one side and answers jumbled down the other. The back of the board has to be set up so that the bulb will light up when the correct question and answer are joined together. Make your game board like this:

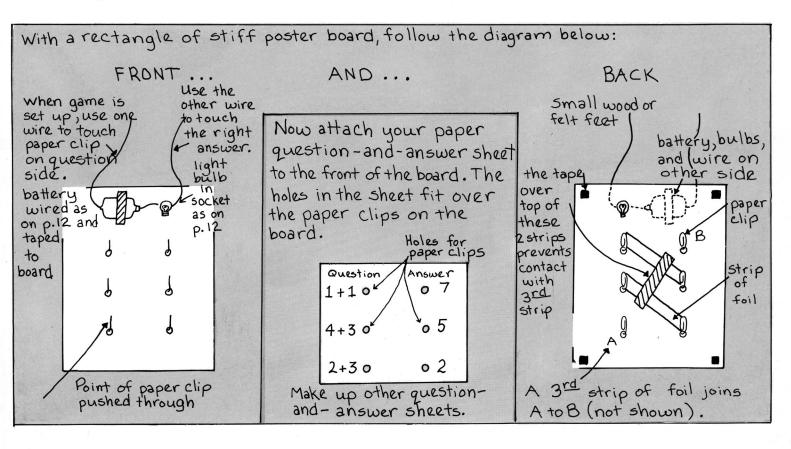

With a rectangle of stiff poster board, follow the diagram below:

FRONT ... AND ... BACK

when game is set up, use one wire to touch paper clip on question side.

Use the other wire to touch the right answer.

battery wired as on p.12 and taped to board

light bulb in socket as on p.12

Point of paper clip pushed through

Now attach your paper question-and-answer sheet to the front of the board. The holes in the sheet fit over the paper clips on the board.

Holes for paper clips

| Question | Answer |
|----------|--------|
| 1+1 o | o 7 |
| 4+3 o | o 5 |
| 2+3 o | o 2 |

Make up other question-and-answer sheets.

Small wood or felt feet

battery, bulbs, and wire on other side

the tape over top of these 2 strips prevents contact with 3rd strip

paper clip

B

Strip of foil

A

A 3rd strip of foil joins A to B (not shown).

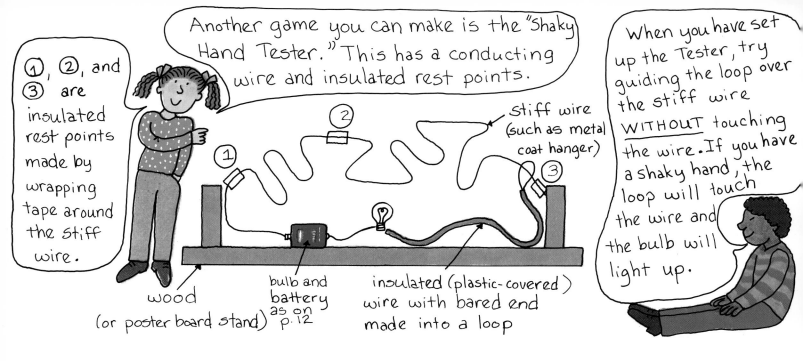

Another game you can make is the "Shaky Hand Tester." This has a conducting wire and insulated rest points.

Not all conductors are equally good at letting electricity pass through them. Wires that let the flow of electricity, the current, pass through easily are called low resistors. Those that it is harder for the current to flow through are called high resistors. Try this experiment with some high-resisting wire. If you pluck some strands from a metal scouring pad, this will give you the wire you need. Wash the soap off it before you use it.

Set up experiment as follows:

ⓐ Take a block of wood and attach the fine wires from the scouring pad to it, using thumbtacks to fix the wires firmly.

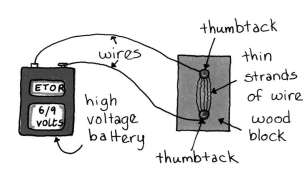

ⓑ Attach a conducting wire to each thumbtack.

ⓒ Now attach the other ends of your conducting wires to the battery. Watch what happens.

The resistance of a wire depends on what it's made of, how long it is and how thin.

The wire in our experiment was very thin and made of iron —so it burned very easily.

Your wire will have burned. All wires get slightly warm when electricity passes through them. The higher their resistance, the warmer they get. The thin wire strands you used in the experiment got so hot that they melted. This could be very dangerous. To stop wires from overheating like this, the main circuit box in a house will have fuses or circuit breakers. If the wiring gets too hot, the fuse will melt or the circuit breaker will click off. These actions stop the flow of current. A fuse is made from a piece of wire that melts easily, like tin. The piece of tin is inside glass so that if it does melt, it can't start a fire.

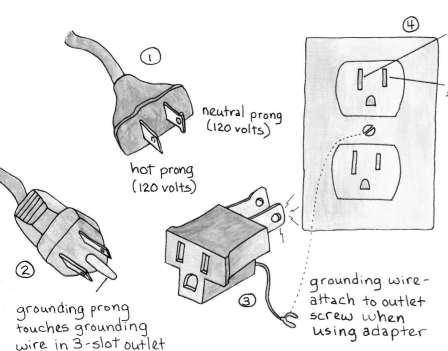

① 

neutral prong (120 volts)

hot prong (120 volts)

② grounding prong touches grounding wire in 3-slot outlet

③ grounding wire— attach to outlet screw when using adapter

④ large slot for neutral prong

small slot for hot prong

① polarized plug
② 3-prong plug
③ 3-prong adapter
④ outlet

TERMS:
grounded wire—current-carrying wire that is grounded at the utility pole for your safety; neutral prong touches it.
ungrounded wire—current-carrying wire that is not grounded; "hot" prong touches this "hot" wire.
adapter—device used to fit a 3-prong plug to a 2-slot outlet.

17

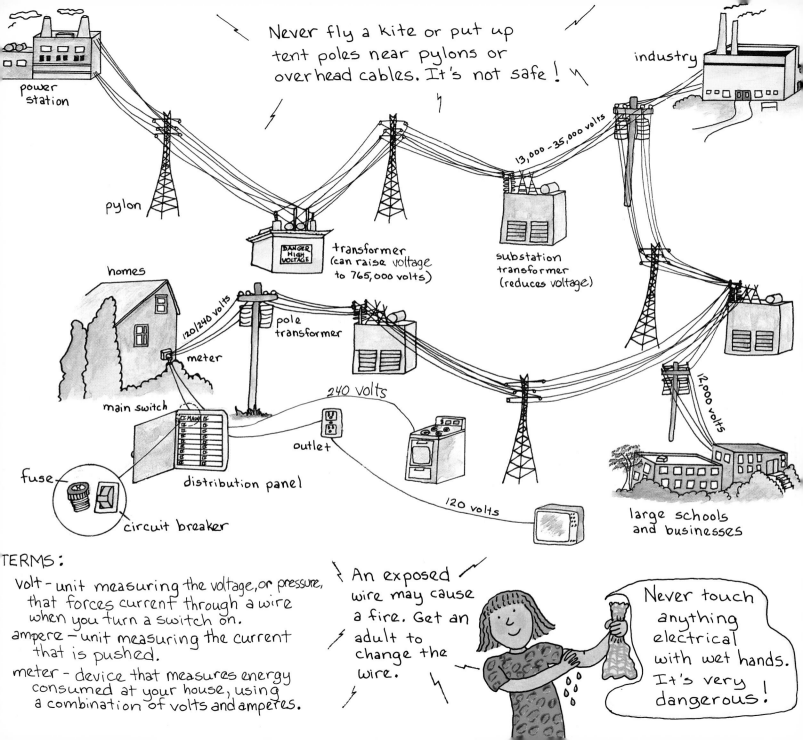

Whenever you switch on an electric space heater or range, you are using this same heating effect. In both of these appliances, part of the circuit is a conductor with a high resistance.

The reason ordinary circuit wire doesn't melt is that it is made of copper, which is a good conductor and does not get too hot. The heating element in your range does get hot, however. It is made from nichrome wire (a combination of nickel and chrome), protected by a ceramic insulating case, and sheathed in metal.

An electric range

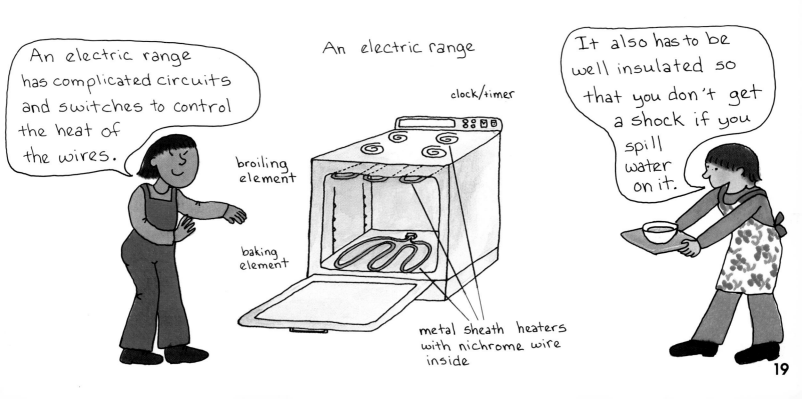

An electric range has complicated circuits and switches to control the heat of the wires.

It also has to be well insulated so that you don't get a shock if you spill water on it.

clock/timer

broiling element

baking element

metal sheath heaters with nichrome wire inside

Over 100 years ago, the first street lamps were lit. They were called electric arc lamps.

Imagine their light as an arc of electricity that glowed as it flowed across a gap of air from one conductor in the bulb to another.

Searchlights and some stagelights we use now are arc lamps, too.

## THE FIRST LIGHT BULBS

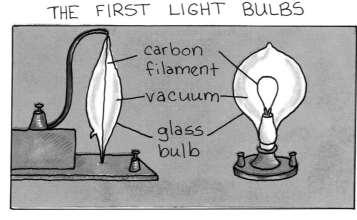

carbon filament
vacuum
glass bulb

The arc lamps of the past had some disadvantages. They became very hot and gave off smoke. A more satisfactory solution was found by Edison and Swan. Their inventions were very similar to the bulb we use today.

Another appliance that uses the heating effect is the light bulb. This was invented at the same time, in 1878, by Thomas Edison in the US and Joseph Swan in Britain. The wire filament that you can see inside a light bulb has a high resistance. It gets so hot that it glows white, giving out light. This filament is made of a metal called tungsten. Although the tungsten will not melt at this great heat, it will react with the oxygen in the air and burn. To stop this from happening, the bulb is filled with a non-reacting gas called argon.

The main difference between Edison's and Swan's bulbs and the modern bulb is that today the vacuum is filled with argon gas.

tungsten wire filament

argon gas

glass support

metal cap

It's gone again!

That means that our bulbs will last a lot longer than Edison's and Swan's.

But sometimes you wouldn't think so.

20

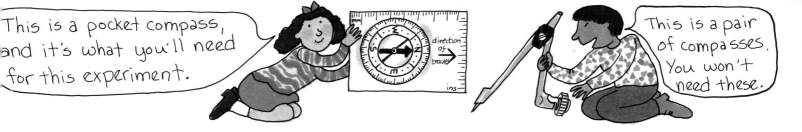

This is a pocket compass, and it's what you'll need for this experiment.

This is a pair of compasses. You won't need these.

Electricity is closely linked to magnetism. To show this, you need a small bar magnet and a compass. If you put the compass near the magnet, it will point in a different direction, instead of pointing north.

The north pole on a bar magnet or compass needle normally points to the North Pole of the Earth if it is allowed to swing freely.

This is strange!

magnet

compass

compass (try it in several positions)

A compass normally points north because the Earth acts as if it has a gigantic magnet inside it.

You can now do the same thing to the compass needle, without using a magnet. Use a 6-volt battery for this or four 1.5-volt ones joined top to bottom. Join a long piece of wire from one battery terminal to the other. Wrap part of the wire tightly around a pencil to make a coil. Pull the pencil out. Now if you put a compass near the coil, the needle will change direction just as it did when it was placed near the magnet.

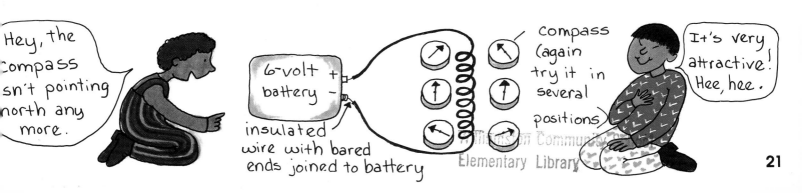

Hey, the compass isn't pointing north any more.

6-volt + battery −

insulated wire with bared ends joined to battery

compass (again try it in several positions)

It's very attractive! Hee, hee.

21

Both the magnet and coil affect the compass because they have a magnetic field around them. This is invisible, but we can see it if we use some iron filings.

Place the magnet under a thin piece of paper, and sprinkle the filings on top of the paper. Give a few gentle taps to the paper, and you will see an interesting pattern start to form. The coil makes the same pattern.

Hold the magnet underneath the paper.

Look what happens. The filings form this pattern.

When you've finished showing the magnetic field, you can have some fun. How? By making funny faces.

Draw a face on a piece of paper. Put some iron filings on the paper, and using the magnet under the paper, move the filings to make a beard, hair, or eyebrows.

The coil you have made could be called an electromagnet. It's not very strong, but if you put an iron nail through the center of the coil, it gets stronger. Try using it to lift up some small iron tacks or nails.

Having more coils will make your magnet stronger. It will pick up more tacks.

battery

6V
EXOR

insulated wire

tacks

iron nail

If you cut off the circuit, the nail will drop the tacks.

Large scrap yards use electromagnets for moving scrap around.

HOSPITAL

Hospitals use them too. Electromagnets can get tiny pieces of iron out of people's eyes.

23

Some animals can also produce magnetic fields. The Mormyrid, a strange-looking fish from Central Africa, can do this. It has eyes that can barely see and a trunk-like snout. In its long, pointed tail it has a group of muscles that can produce electricity in short pulses, making its tail negative and its head positive. This produces a magnetic field around the fish, which the fish uses to sense objects around it as it moves.

"|₁" is the electrical symbol for a battery cell. "|₁|₁" is two cells.

It makes life easier for the lazy diagram artist.

The first electromagnet was made in England by William Sturgeon in 1825. You can use your electromagnet to make an electric bell. Here is one way of doing it:

bent paper clip

thumb tacks

wood stand (with nail taped on)

can or old bell top
metal lump (taped on)
piece of iron
plastic ruler
heavy object such as a brick

tap switch
touch thumb tack with the end of the bent paper clip

batteries |₁|₁

When you tap the switch, the circuit is complete, and the nail is magnetized. This attracts the iron piece and bends the ruler, banging the metal lump against the can or bell top. It rings. Take your finger off the switch. The nail releases and the ruler swings back.

The American Samuel Morse used an electromagnet when he invented the telegraph in 1837. This had a buzzer that worked rather like your bell. Of course, to send messages over large distances, the wires between the buzzer and tap switch had to be hundreds of miles long.

THE MORSE CODE

| A | B | C | D | E | F | G | H | I | J | K | L | M |
|---|---|---|---|---|---|---|---|---|---|---|---|---|
| ·— | —··· | —·—· | —·· | · | ··—· | ——· | ···· | ·· | ·——— | —·— | ·—·· | —— |

| N | O | P | Q | R | S | T | U | V | W | X | Y | Z |
|---|---|---|---|---|---|---|---|---|---|---|---|---|
| —· | ——— | ·——· | ——·— | ·—· | ··· | — | ··— | ···— | ·—— | —··— | —·—— | ——·· |

25

When you speak to someone on the phone, an electric signal goes from the mouthpiece. It travels along wires to the other telephone...

earpiece (receiver) electromagnets

...where it works the earpiece so that the other person hears you. Then it talks back to you in the same way.

sound waves

mouthpiece (microphone)

Although it's more complicated than the telegraph, the telephone works in a similar way, using electromagnets. This was developed in the US by Alexander Graham Bell in 1876. Earlier in the 19th century, another scientist, Michael Faraday, had found a way of using magnetism to make electricity, which led to the invention of the electric generator in 1831.

Michael Faraday was particularly famous for his experiments in physics. This picture shows Faraday with the first electric generator.

Faraday was also professor of chemistry at the Royal Institution, London, for thirty years. Scientists sometimes called him "the father of electricity."

disc

coil

Why aren't the lights working?

It's obvious. With a generator, you **must** keep cycling for the lights to stay on.

Some bicycles have generators instead of batteries to provide power for the lights. Unlike a battery, a generator doesn't run out, but if you stop moving, the lights go out. Inside a generator, there is a magnet, bent so both poles face inward. Between the poles is a coil of wire. If the wire coil is moved by the turning of the bicycle wheel, then electricity starts to flow through the wire.

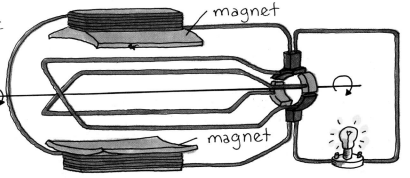

In a simple electric generator, a coil of wire is turned clockwise by mechanical energy (you moving the pedals).

magnet

magnet

The coil lies between opposite poles (N and S) of two magnets. This causes a flow of electric current in the coil as it rotates and lights the bulb.

Inside power stations, there are huge generators that make vast amounts of electricity. They are driven by steam engines fueled by oil, coal, or nuclear power.

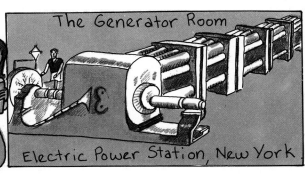

The Generator Room

Electric Power Station, New York

It was many years after Faraday's discovery before the results of his work were used. But in 1882 things were to change.

Thomas A. Edison built the first large power station in New York. Others were built in England. At last there was power to the people.

If you have a toy electric train or car at home, open it up and look inside. You will see what looks like a generator. In fact, it's an electric motor. A motor is just a generator used in a different way. In a generator, you turn a wire coil inside a magnetic field to make electricity. In a motor, you pass electricity through the wire coil and it spins. Motors like this can be powerful enough to turn the wheels on a vehicle the size of a golf cart or fork lift.

The generator made large amounts of electricity available for the first time. Inventors soon began to put this to use. The telegraph and telephone inventions were followed by Edison's phonograph, an early record player, in 1877. And in 1878, British physicist William Crookes invented the cathode ray tube that we now use in TV.

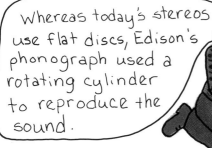

Whereas today's stereos use flat discs, Edison's phonograph used a rotating cylinder to reproduce the sound.

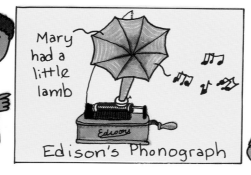

Mary had a little lamb

Edison's Phonograph

The very first recording was the words of the nursery rhyme, "Mary had a little lamb. Its fleece was white as snow."

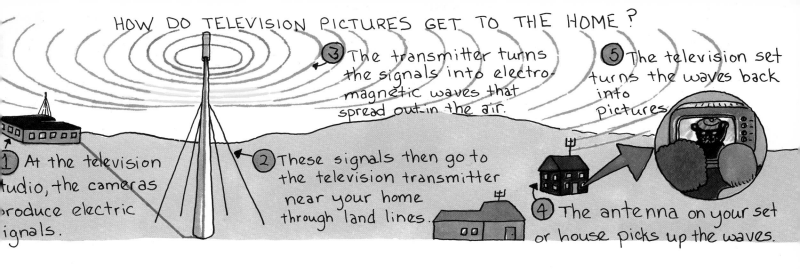

## HOW DO TELEVISION PICTURES GET TO THE HOME?

③ The transmitter turns the signals into electro-magnetic waves that spread out in the air.

⑤ The television set turns the waves back into pictures.

① At the television studio, the cameras produce electric signals.

② These signals then go to the television transmitter near your home through land lines.

④ The antenna on your set or house picks up the waves.

In Italy, Guglielmo Marconi revolutionized message-sending with the invention of the radio in 1895. The radio depends on electromagnetic waves. Of course, many other scientists were involved in this work. Their inventions and discoveries eventually allowed John Logie Baird in Britain and Vladimir Zworykin in the US to develop a way of sending pictures by electromagnetic waves. This was television.

It would be difficult for you to make a TV or radio transmitter in your home, but you can use electricity to send messages — like this:

Set up a simple circuit with a battery, a bulb, and a tap switch. Send messages to your friend, using the Morse code on page 25.

A short tap on the tap switch means a dot, and long tap is a dash.

What on earth is he saying?

They're using Volta's battery, Edison's lamp, and Morse's code to send messages to one another.

Try inventing your own code.

A microchip is pretty small. Take a look at this!

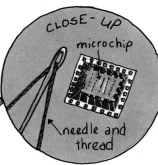

CLOSE-UP

microchip

needle and thread

The invention of microchips has enabled computers to become more powerful, smaller and cheaper to run.

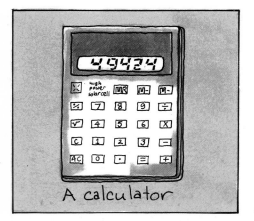

A calculator

Since the 1940s, and especially in the last ten years, there has been a further revolution in the use of electricity with the development of electronic and microelectronic circuits. These work basically in the same way as the electric circuits you have been using, but they are extremely small. They are so small, in fact, that hundreds of them could be fit into an area the size of a postage stamp. These circuits are printed on silicon and so are called silicon chips or microchips.

A video recorder

A digital watch

Think of everyday objects that use microchips.

Please fasten your seat belts. Thank You!

A "speaking" car dashboard

Here are some examples.

Electronics has allowed the development of many new tools and machines. One of the most important of these is the new generation of computers that use tiny circuits called integrated circuits. These can store, use, and process information at incredible speed. More and more people are learning to use computers. Microcomputers are finding their way into many homes. With all these exciting developments taking place, we can barely imagine how we will use electricity in the future!

## Glossary

**Conductor:** something that lets electricity flow through it, like metals and water.

**Electrical circuit:** a path that electricity can take without being stopped.

**Electromagnet:** a current-carrying device with a soft-iron core surrounded by insulating wire; the current causes the magnet to attract objects.

**Electron:** a particle that orbits the nucleus of an atom; those materials that best conduct electricity have free electrons, that is, electrons that move.

**Fuse:** a device on an electric wire; it prevents fires by melting when a wire is overloaded, thereby breaking the circuit of electricity.

**Generator:** a device that turns mechanical energy into electrical energy.

**High resistors:** those conductors that do not easily accept the flow of electricity.

**Insulator:** something that will not let electricity flow through it, like paper, rubber, and plastic.

**Lightning:** sparks that leap through the air; made up of electrical charges that occur when particles of water, ice, and air rub together in clouds.

**Lightning rod:** a metal rod extending 2 feet above structures; it is attached to a grounded cable.

**Low resistors:** those conductors that electricity flows through easily.

**Transformer:** something that transfers electricity from one circuit to another; transformers can both raise power so that it travels quickly over great distances or reduce it so that it can safely enter industry, stores, and homes.

**Volt:** a unit of measurement telling how much electrical pressure is forcing current through a conductor; a large industry might need 35,000 volts while homes need only 120/240 volts.

**Watt:** a unit of measure indicating electrical power; the wattage of an appliance, for example, is an indicator of how much power it needs to run. A **kilowatt** is 1,000 watts.

**Watthour:** a unit of measure indicating how much power is needed to run something at the rate of one watt per hour; a 60-watt light bulb burning for 1 hour uses 60 watthours of electricity. Our electric bills are based on watthours.

## Index